How Digital Communications Changed the World

Stephanie Feldstein

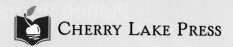

CHERRY LAKE PRESS

Published in the United States of America by Cherry Lake Publishing Group
Ann Arbor, Michigan
www.cherrylakepublishing.com

Reading Adviser: Beth Walker Gambro, MS, Ed., Reading Consultant, Yorkville, IL

Photo Credits: © PradeepGaurs/Shutterstock, cover; © Ksenia Ragozina/Shutterstock, 4; © Gorodenkoff/Shutterstock, 6; LSE Library, No restrictions, via Wikimedia Commons, 9; © Artie Medvedev/Shutterstock, 10; © Studio Romantic/ Shutterstock, 11; © Marcel Antonisse / Anefo, CC0, via Wikimedia Commons, 12; © Akhenaton Images/Shutterstock, 13; © Ruslana Iurchenko/Shutterstock, 14; © Twin Design/Shutterstock, 15; © Agnes Kantaruk/Shutterstock, 16; © Rawpixel.com/Shutterstock, 17; © alexjey/Shutterstock, 19; © Cavan-Images/Shutterstock, 20; © Natalia de la Rubia/Shutterstock, 21; © OlegDoroshin/Shutterstock, 22; © aslysun/Shutterstock, 25; © ra2 studio/Shutterstock, 26; © myboys.me/Shutterstock, 27; © Deemerwha studio, 28; © TierneyMJ/Shutterstock, 29; © II.studio/Shutterstock, 30

Cherry Lake Press is an imprint of Cherry Lake Publishing Group.

Library of Congress Cataloging-in-Publication Data

Names: Feldstein, Stephanie, author.
Title: How digital communications changed the world / Written by: Stephanie Feldstein.
Description: Ann Arbor, Michigan : Cherry Lake Publishing, 2024. | Series: Planet human | Audience: Grades 4-6 |
    Summary: "The digital communications industry has profoundly impacted our world. The Planet Human series
    breaks down the human impact on the environment over time and around the globe. Each title presents important
    high-interest natural science nonfiction content with global relevance"— Provided by publisher.
Identifiers: LCCN 2023035100 | ISBN 9781668939055 (paperback) | ISBN 9781668938010 (hardcover) |
    ISBN 9781668940396 (ebook) | ISBN 9781668941744 (pdf)
Subjects: LCSH: Internet—Juvenile literature. | Digital communications—Juvenile literature.
Classification: LCC HM851 .F455 2024 | DDC 004.6—dc23/eng/20230807
LC record available at https://lccn.loc.gov/2023035100

Cherry Lake Publishing Group would like to acknowledge the work of the Partnership for 21st Century Learning, a Network of Battelle for Kids. Please visit Battelle for Kids online for more information.

Printed in the United States of America

Note from publisher: Websites change regularly, and their future contents are outside of our control. Supervise children when conducting any recommended online searches for extended learning opportunities.

Stephanie Feldstein works at the Center for Biological Diversity. She advocates to protect wildlife and helps people understand how humans impact nature. She lives in the woods in the Pacific Northwest with her rescued dogs and cats. She loves to hike and explore wild places.

CONTENTS

Introduction

Lithium Flats

South America is home to one of the world's most unique regions. This region is known as the Lithium Triangle. It sits between Argentina, Bolivia, and Chile. It is rich in rare minerals. It has salt lakes and salt flats. It has wetlands full of **biodiversity**. Pumas, foxes, and armadillos live there. So do colorful flamingos. It's home to some of the oldest life forms on the planet. And it's also home to miles of **lithium** mines. Some are so huge they can be seen from space.

Lithium is mined by pulling brine from deep underground. Brine is water with lots of minerals. It's stored in ponds. Chemicals are used to dry the ponds. The water evaporates. Lithium is left behind. Pumping water from the ground affects the **habitat** where wild animals live. It takes water from local communities.

A Giant Industry

About 5 billion people use the internet. That's close to two-thirds of all people in the world. And it's still growing. Originally, experts thought less than half the world would be online today. We've already passed that. Now it's estimated that 90 percent of people will be online by 2030.

The internet is run by huge data centers. They're filled with computers called servers. Servers store the information found online. They transmit data from one place to another. The average data center is as big as two football fields. Some are much bigger. They can be millions of square feet. They can use as much energy as a medium-sized town.

Lithium is the lightest metal on Earth. It's used in rechargeable batteries. It's used to power electric cars. It's also used to power smartphones and laptops. **Digital communication** depends on it.

Web pages, texting, email, and social media are all digital communications. They help us get and share information. They connect people around the world.

Producing and powering our devices is a huge **industry**. And it has grown very quickly.

Human industry has changed the face of the planet. More than 8 billion people live on Earth. People are living longer. We're healthier than ever. But everything we use or buy comes at a cost. Human industry uses natural resources that wildlife needs. It creates **pollution** and waste. It can affect human health, too. Our industries put a lot of pressure on nature. The most pressure comes from wealthy countries like the United States.

We need a healthy planet to survive. We need clean air and safe water. We need **ecosystems** with lots of different wildlife. Digital communication has a huge impact on nature and society. We can make sure its future is good for people and the planet.

CHAPTER 1

The History of Digital Communications

It's hard to imagine life without mobile phones. More people have mobile phones than toilets. But mobile phones didn't exist until 50 years ago. They were big and clunky. And they could only be used for calls. The first text message wasn't sent until December 1992. It said, "Merry Christmas."

The first computers were massive. They took up entire rooms. It took teams of engineers to keep them running. But smaller computer chips were invented in the 1970s. They were called microprocessors. They were the size of a thumbnail. It made smaller computers possible. People started to have personal computers at home.

A student uses a personal computer in the 1970s.

The earliest personal computers could do calculations. They could be used to play simple games. But they couldn't do much else. By the 1980s, more programs were developed. The technology got better and faster. And computers kept getting smaller. Personal computers eventually led to today's laptops. They opened the door for smartphones and tablets.

People used computers to talk to each other as early as the 1960s. Researchers were already imagining a vast network.

Digital Communications and Human Health

People in the United States spend more than 8 hours a day online. That's about 150 percent more than a decade ago. Spending a lot of time online can affect people's health. Staring at screens can cause eye strain. Hunching over devices can cause neck pain. Online use can prevent people from getting enough exercise. It can cause sleep problems.

Social media can affect mental health. Studies have linked it to anxiety and loneliness. It's been linked to depression. But other studies have shown the opposite. Some people find social support online. They have fewer mental health problems. It affects different people in different ways.

The internet has improved health, too. It's made it easier for people to receive health care. They can chat with a doctor or nurse from home.

Kids at a computer festival in the Netherlands in 1984.

Back in the 1980s, being able to access the internet with a handheld device was a far-off dream.

They wanted people to access information from anywhere. Email was mostly used by researchers. But by the 1980s, the technology moved beyond the lab. Businesses and people started to use it. In 1995, the term *internet* was officially adopted.

The first recorded social media site launched in 1997. Social media wasn't very popular at first. In 2005, only 5 percent of Americans were on social media. Today, more than 70 percent use it. It's transformed the way we interact with each other. It's transformed how we interact with the world.

THE DIGITAL DIVIDE

Most Americans have internet access at home. But it's not equal. It varies based on income. About 97 percent of wealthy Americans have smartphones. More than 90 percent have high-speed internet. But only 76 percent of Americans with low incomes have smartphones. Only 57 percent have fast internet at home. Access can also vary based on race. It can vary based on where you live.

This gap is called the **digital divide**. It affects who can access information. It makes it harder for people to find jobs. It's harder for children to do their homework. It worsens inequality.

There is a debate going on about social media. People are trying to decide if it is healthy or unhealthy.

It used to take much longer to send and receive messages. Letters were how people shared news and caught up with friends.

Now people can send and receive emails in a matter of seconds.

Digital communication was developed to connect people. It's about sharing ideas and information. People used to have to wait weeks or months for a letter to arrive. Now an email or text arrives almost instantly. We can access more information than ever before. And it will only continue to get faster.

CHAPTER 2

The Environmental Cost of Digital Communications

It may not seem like sending a text or email affects the environment. But digital communications run on energy. More than 1 percent of the world's electricity is used by data centers. Most of that energy comes from **fossil fuels**. Fossil fuels cause environmental damage. They drive **climate change**. Climate change affects all life on Earth. It causes extreme weather. It changes ecosystems. It puts people and wildlife in danger.

Around 350 billion emails are sent every day. The energy needed for them creates climate pollution.

Oil, coal, and natural gas are fossil fuels.

Brine pools are used for lithium mining. Lithium mining can release chemicals and heavy metals into surrounding air and water.

Almost as much energy is used making devices as in using them. Devices have parts made of precious metals like lithium. Mining those metals creates **toxic** pollution. It uses a lot of water. It destroys ecosystems. It harms wildlife. Devices also have plastic parts. Plastic is made with toxic chemicals. It makes climate change worse.

Electronics that are thrown away are called **e-waste**. E-waste harms people and the environment. It's not **biodegradable**. Electronics don't break down in nature. They just keep piling up. They also contain toxic materials. They can poison soil and wildlife. They can pollute air and water. They can harm workers and communities. Recycling can help safely dispose of harmful materials.

Changemaker: Aza Raskin

Aza Raskin invented technology used in social media. But he realized it made people more addicted to their devices. So he cofounded the Center for Humane Technology in 2018. It works for technology that improves well-being.

Raskin also started the Earth Species Project. It uses computers to decode animal language. The computer doesn't understand the words. But it looks for patterns. That's how the computer translates similar words.

The Earth Species Project collects sounds from nature. It records all kinds of animal species. These include crows and dolphins. The computer will need a lot of data. Then it can try to map out the languages.

But Raskin says the project isn't really about talking. It's more about listening. Listening can help us better understand animals. And that can help us better protect them.

One of the most common reasons for replacing
a smartphone is a lowered battery performance.
Another common reason is screen damage.

Recycling electronics also helps reclaim precious metals. It's much less destructive than mining. It saves energy. It reduces waste. But only 17 percent of all electronics are recycled. People are working to pass laws that would require recycling. They would require safe disposal of electronics.

Devices can be made to last longer. That would reduce the resources needed. It would help prevent e-waste. There are also better ways to mine for precious metals. The industry wants the fastest, cheapest way to get the metals. But there are ways that cause less harm. People don't need to mine where sensitive wildlife lives.

THE IMPACT OF SMARTPHONES

Smartphones are the most popular electronic devices in the world. People tend to replace them often. There are about 16 billion mobile phones in the world. That's enough for every person on the planet to have two.

People in wealthy countries used to keep their phones for fewer than 2 years. That's starting to change. Phones are lasting longer. Companies are providing more support. Waiting to replace phones reduces e-waste. It reduces their environmental impact.

CHAPTER 3

From Science Fiction to Reality

Years ago, people wrote science fiction stories about pocket-sized computers. Now we carry around smartphones more powerful than any computer they could have imagined. And it's not just our phones that are smart. Smart thermostats regulate temperatures in buildings. Smart mirrors let you see information like the weather forecast. Smart refrigerators let you see what's inside. You can order food without even opening the door.

More and more devices are getting "smart." Smart devices are electronics that network with other devices. It could be a dog collar that links to your phone. Or a toaster connected to the internet. Together, these devices are called the Internet of Things.

Smart technology gathers and shares information between devices. It can be fun to turn on lights from

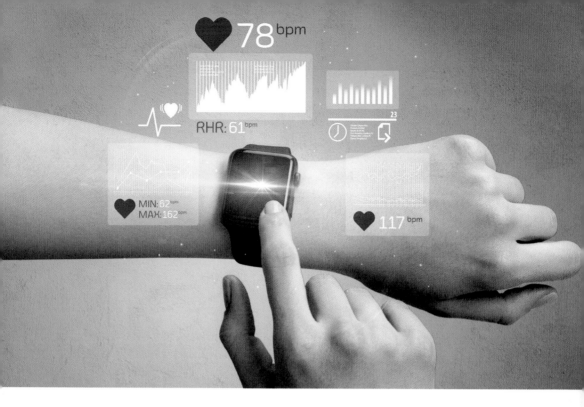

Smart watches are another device that can help monitor people's health.

another room. But it's about more than just cool features. Smart homes can sense medical emergencies and get people help faster. Smart technology collects data fast. It makes it easier for people to use that data.

The Internet of Things is changing how we interact with our stuff. And smart devices keep getting smarter. They make it easier for people to access information. They're changing every industry. They're making factories safer

They're helping farmers monitor crops. They're helping doctors take better care of patients.

But smart devices can have a larger environmental impact. Adding computer chips to everyday items uses more resources. A smart toaster has more rare metals and electronics than a regular toaster. And technology changes quickly. Replacing outdated devices creates e-waste.

THE IMPACT OF SOCIAL MEDIA

Social media is an important tool to protect the environment. It helps people connect for climate protests. It helps people better understand science. It also helps them see how incredible nature is. It helps people learn about wildlife. It inspires them to want to save the planet.

But social media can have a dark side, too. It can be used to trick or mislead people. It can be used for bullying. It can expose people to harmful content. Are the negative impacts of social media on people worth the positive impact on environmental action? Should there be more laws to improve online safety?

The Future of Digital Communications

Artificial intelligence, or AI, is the ability for computers to think and learn.

AI is already used in many ways. But it's still developing. It's getting better at understanding language. It can create realistic images. It can create text that could have been written by a human.

There are many benefits to AI. It can process much more information quicker than people can. It can help researchers analyze environmental data. That can help them figure out how to best protect wildlife. It can help people take action to stop pollution. It also makes simple tasks easier.

AI can be dangerous, too. Sometimes it gets things wrong. It can create false information that looks real. AI also doesn't know right from wrong. It doesn't have real-life experiences and feelings. Those help us make good decisions. AI could mislead people about environmental solutions. Bad information can lead to decisions that harm people and the planet.

Cybersecurity is a growing field. More and more people are looking to keep their personal information private online.

But companies can take responsibility for their smart devices. They can build them to last longer. They can make sure they're properly recycled.

Smart technology can also make devices more **efficient**. Efficient devices use less energy to do the same job. They reduce the impact of technology on the environment. A smart dishwasher will use less water and energy even when it's not full.

People—and things—being connected has many benefits. But there is a risk that smart devices can share too much data. The wrong people could access it. People have a right to keep their information private. That privacy needs to be protected. Companies can make sure smart devices stay safe. The Internet of Things should make our lives easier without causing harm.

Activity

Give Websites the CRAAP Test

CRAAP stands for currency, relevance, authority, accuracy, and purpose. These five things can help you evaluate what you're reading. It can help you spot false information online. Choose an environmental topic to research. For example, look up ways to help wildlife.

Go online with an adult. Type your research topic into a search engine. Choose a link that looks interesting. Then use the CRAAP test:

1. **Currency.** Look for a date on the webpage. Is it recent? If not, the information might no longer be true. It might be missing the latest updates.

2. **Relevancy.** Is it related to your topic? Or does it only mention it once? Look for sites with lots of information about your topic.

3. **Accuracy.** Is the information correct? Does it link to sources? Watch out for claims that aren't backed up by facts. Check facts against other sources. If the facts don't match up, don't trust the website.

4. **Authority.** Look for the "about" page or author bio. Who wrote the information? Are they an environmental expert? Do they work or study in the field?

5. **Purpose.** What kind of website is it? Is it educational? Is it just for entertainment? Skip sites from businesses trying to sell something. Look for sites from scientists who know about wildlife. Look for groups working to protect the planet.

Did the website pass the CRAAP test?

An official website of the United States government

EPA United States Environmental Protection Agency

Environmental Topics

s & Regul

Learn More

Books

Grant, Joyce. *Can You Believe It?: How to Spot Fake News and Find the Facts.* Toronto, ON: Kids Can Press, 2022.

Hawkins, Carole. *STEAM Jobs in Internet Technology.* Greensboro, NC: Rourke Educational Media, 2019.

Sichol, Lowey Bundy. *From an Idea to Google: How Innovation at Google Changed the World.* New York, NY: Clarion Books, 2019.

Truesdell, Ann. *How to Handle Cyberbullies.* Ann Arbor, MI: Cherry Lake Publishing, 2014.

On the Web

With an adult, learn more online with these suggested searches.

"Electronic waste facts for kids" — Kiddle

"What is E-WASTE Pollution? | What Causes Electronic Waste? | The Dr. Binocs Show | Peekaboo Kidz" — YouTube

"What Really Happens to Our Old Electronics?" Video — Above the Noise/KQED

Glossary

artificial intelligence (ar-tuh-FIH-shuhl in-TEH-luh-juhnts) or AI (AY IYE) the ability for computers to think and learn

biodegradable (biye-oh-dih-GRAY-duh-buhl) capable of being broken down in the environment

biodiversity (biye-oh-dih-VUHR-suh-tee) the variety of plants and animals in nature

climate change (KLIYE-muht CHAYNJ) changes in weather, temperatures, and other natural conditions over time

digital communication (DIH-juh-tuhl kuh-myoo-nuh-KAY-shuhn) using technology to talk to each other

digital divide (DIH-juh-tuhl duh-VIYED) the difference in access to digital communications based on income, race, or location

ecosystems (EE-koh-sih-stuhmz) places where plants, animals, and the environment rely on each other

efficient (ih-FIH-shuhnt) using less energy to do the same jobs.

e-waste (EE-wayst) electronics that are thrown away

fossil fuels (FAH-suhl FYOOLZ) fuels like oil, gas, and coal that come from the remains of plants and animals and are burned for energy

habitat (HAB-uh-tat) the natural home of plants and animals

industry (IN-duh-stree) all the companies that make and sell a kind of product or service

lithium (LIH-thee-uhm) a lightweight metal used in battery-powered devices like electric cars, mobile phones, and laptops

pollution (puh-LOO-shuhn) harmful materials released into the environment

toxic (TAHK-sik) something that is harmful or poisonous

Index